Presented To

_____

From

_____

Date

_____

The Speckled Egg Principle™

The Speckled Egg Principle™

Discovering, Nurturing, and Leveraging the Uniquely Gifted Leader

Carol J. Cline

Copyright © 2016 – Carol J. Cline

All rights reserved. No part of this book may be used or reproduced in any manner, stored in a retrieval system, or transmitted in any form or by any means—electronic, mechanical, photocopy, recording, scanning or any other—except in the case of brief quotations in printed reviews, without the prior written permission from the author.

Scotland Media Group
3583 Scotland Road Building 70
Scotland OPA 17254

Book ISBN: 978-1-941746-32-5

eBook ISBN: 978-1-941746-33-0

For Worldwide Distribution
Printed in the United States

1 2 3 4 5 6 7 / 20 19 18 17 16

Dedication

Dedicated to my parents, Russ and Angie (Godbold) Newell, who encouraged me to listen to my heart, discover my talents, develop my skills, and always come home to the grace that sustains us all.

The meaning of life is to find your gift.
The purpose of life is to give it away.

—William Shakespeare

The Speckled Egg Principle™

Speckled eggs are the talents, gifts, and skills hidden under the wings of your organization that—when discovered and nurtured—will help your organization soar.

Contents

Introduction	*xiii*
How to Use this Book	*xv*
Questions 1-100	*1*
Hatched	*101*
Incubate	*103*
Nurture	*105*
Treasure Mapping and IT	*107*
Conclusion	*109*
About the Author	*111*

Introduction

Speckled eggs can be found in every person…in every organization. These "eggs" are untapped resources waiting to be called upon and empowered to add value beyond expectations. A culture that identifies and celebrates individual talents and strengths at every level will experience a collision of personal satisfaction and maximum contribution. The result? Engaged and empowered individuals living their passion. An organization that soars.

A deeper understanding of a person's giftedness increases the opportunity for tailored development. In an era where more is to be accomplished using fewer resources, validating and repositioning talents already employed seems not only reasonable, but prudent. Having the right person in the right position and doing the right thing at the right time for the right reason is critical to an individual's success and the overall health of the organization.

Everyone has value. That is absolutely true. Whether or not people contribute their value is dependent on proper alignment of individual talent with the expectations of their role. Does the role (what they do) provide purpose and meaning (what they love) and reflect who they are (what they value and believe)?

Given a choice, most individuals prefer to invest their time in ways that provide meaning and purpose. They seek opportunities to live their passion.

Developing talent within the organization is vital. The challenge for you as a leader is creating margins for your own personal development. It is important for leaders to prioritize time to refresh, recharge, and refocus.

Grant yourself permission to be still and reflect on who and what matters most in your life. You must first care for yourself in order to have the strength and courage to serve others.

As you begin, you will find that what brought you this far matters. Many of your answers to the following questions will reveal new possibilities and opportunities. You may establish or rekindle talents and gifts that lead you toward fresh adventures.

The process of reflection will help you discover, or affirm, what you treasure, how you are gifted, and the desires of your heart.

Today is the day.

This is your journey.

How to Use this Book

Throughout your journey you will learn more about yourself as you answer the questions. You will also log your talents, skills, and gifts on the HATCHED, INCUBATE, and/or NURTURE pages in the back of the book.

Before you begin to answer the questions that follow, think about the talents, skills, and gifts you currently use in leadership roles. Then enter those on the HATCHED page.

There are 100 thought provoking questions in no particular order. Some answers may take considerable time, thought, and reflection. I suggest you review all of the questions and then select a dozen or so that are most relevant to your journey. You can use the eggs at the bottom of the page to mark them so they are easy to find. Answer those questions first.

As your answers reveal additional talents, skills, gifts, or interests, write those on the INCUBATE page.

After the questions you selected are answered, compare your entries on HATCHED and INCUBATE pages. On the NURTURE page, enter the talents, skills, and gifts that you want to develop.

You have then identified your speckled eggs that represent ways you are uniquely gifted. You will refer to them in the *Treasure Mapping* process later in the book.

Let your journey begin. Sit back. Breathe deeply.

Open yourself to new insights and possibilities.

Some of the questions you are about to ask yourself are easy… a relative "walk in the park." Your answers require little reflection. Other questions will stir rediscovery of talents and gifts that have yielded to daily demands. And some questions will take more time.

Allow each question to linger in your mind. Your answers will move beyond convenient and superficial. They will prompt you to look for deeper connections between what you do, what you love, and who you are.

Answer the questions that are important to you.

Allow time for honest consideration.

Only you have the answers.

There are no wrong answers.

The Speckled Egg Principle™

Question 1

How will someone's life be different because you spoke with that person today?

_____
_____
_____
_____
_____
_____
_____
_____
_____
_____
_____
_____
_____
_____
_____
_____

Question 2

What achievement are you most proud of? Did you celebrate it? With whom? How did it affect you?

The Speckled Egg Principle™

Question 3

What is your youngest memory? How old were you?

Question 4

How do you spend the majority of your day? Is this by choice or another person's expectation?

___

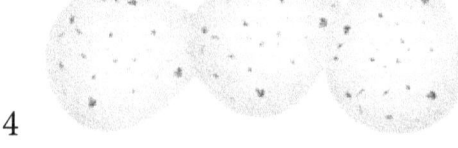

Question 5

List five leadership characteristics that are important to you. Number them 1-5 (#1 most important). Do you consider #1 the cornerstone of your leadership style?

___
___
___
___
___
___
___
___
___
___
___
___
___
___
___
___

Question 6

How would you describe the community in which you live? What do you enjoy about living there?

_____
_____
_____
_____
_____
_____
_____
_____
_____
_____
_____
_____
_____
_____
_____

The Speckled Egg Principle™

Question 7

Are there things you can quit doing to have time for something different or new?

Question 8

What is your greatest joy?

Question 9

Does a person's status or title change how you interact with that person? Should it? Why or why not?

Question 10

What is your favorite pastime and when was the last time you participated in it?

The Speckled Egg Principle™

Question 11

How would you like to spend a rainy day?

Question 12

If your neighbor, co-worker, or family member were to describe you, what would each say?

___
___
___
___
___
___
___
___
___
___
___
___
___
___

The Speckled Egg Principle™

Question 13

What do you love about your work? What percent of each day are you doing what you love?

Question 14

Who makes a difference in your life? How?

The Speckled Egg Principle™

Question 15

Who do you admire? Which of their attributes would you like to develop in yourself?

_____
_____
_____
_____
_____
_____
_____
_____
_____
_____
_____
_____
_____
_____

Question 16

What is your pet peeve?

_____
_____
_____
_____
_____
_____
_____
_____
_____
_____
_____
_____
_____
_____
_____

The Speckled Egg Principle™

Question 17

When have you experienced compassion?

Question 18

If you owned the company where you work, would you hire you? Why?

_____

_____

_____

_____

_____

_____

_____

_____

_____

_____

_____

_____

_____

_____

The Speckled Egg Principle™

Question 19

What have you done today to feed your soul?

_____

_____

_____

_____

_____

_____

_____

_____

_____

_____

_____

_____

_____

_____

_____

Question 20

What books have you read in the past month? Which would you recommend to a friend and why?

The Speckled Egg Principle™

Question 21

What is the difference between a boss and a leader? Which are you?

Question 22

What is your learning style? Is it difficult to adapt to an alternate style?

The Speckled Egg Principle™

Question 23

What makes you get up in the morning?

Question 24

Where is your happy place?

The Speckled Egg Principle™

Question 25

What one thing would you change to make your environments more positive?

Question 26

What songs make you dance?

Question 27

What is your greatest fear? How does it paralyze or motivate you?

Question 28

Do you actively listen? Can you detect the unspoken? How do you ensure understanding?

Question 29

What do you do regularly to keep your mind, body, and spirit healthy?

_____
_____
_____
_____
_____
_____
_____
_____
_____
_____
_____
_____
_____
_____
_____

Question 30

In what circumstances are you most likely to use the words "always" or "never"?

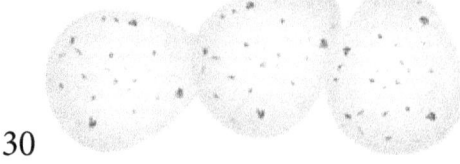

The Speckled Egg Principle™

Question 31

What talent would you like others to know you have?

_____

_____

_____

_____

_____

_____

_____

_____

_____

_____

_____

_____

_____

Question 32

How do you define family?

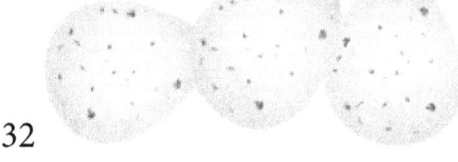

Question 33

What are your top personal and professional goals in the next six months?

Question 34

With whom do you share your vision?

The Speckled Egg Principle™

Question 35

What is your next BIG idea?

Question 36

Who are your biggest fans? How do they show their support?

_____
_____
_____
_____
_____
_____
_____
_____
_____
_____
_____
_____
_____
_____

The Speckled Egg Principle™

Question 37

How do you encourage others?

_____
_____
_____
_____
_____
_____
_____
_____
_____
_____
_____
_____
_____
_____
_____

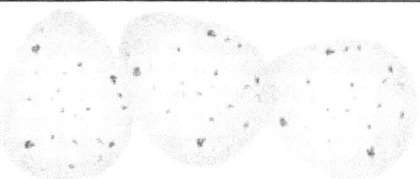

Question 38

If you could instantly change one thing about yourself, what would it be? Why?

Question 39

What makes you run away?

Question 40

How do you affect the bottom line?

Question 41

What is your greatest strength?

Question 42

Are you truly happy? How can others tell if you are happy or not?

The Speckled Egg Principle™

Question 43

Where would you like to be right now?

Question 44

What is your ideal vacation?

_____
_____
_____
_____
_____
_____
_____
_____
_____
_____
_____
_____
_____
_____
_____
_____
_____

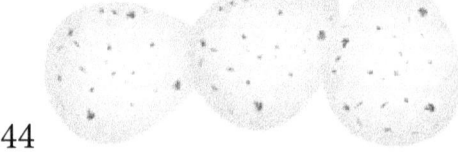

Question 45

What is your favorite type of music? How often do you listen to it?

Question 46

What do you treasure?

_____
_____
_____
_____
_____
_____
_____
_____
_____
_____
_____
_____
_____
_____
_____

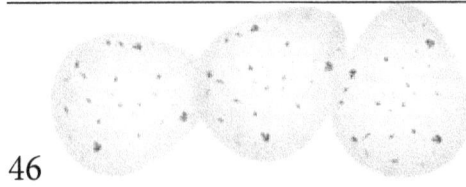

Question 47

Who do you treasure? Do they know?

Question 48

How do you describe a good day? At work? At home? At play?

Question 49

What three words best describe you?

Question 50

If you had time each week to volunteer, where would you invest your time and talents?

Question 51

What makes you feel most stressed? How do you deal with it in that moment?

Question 52

On a scale from 1-10, how would you rate your work/life balance? Are you where you want to be?

The Speckled Egg Principle™

Question 53

If you could design your perfect job, what would it look like?

Question 54

If you could shadow anyone for one day, who would you choose? Why?

The Speckled Egg Principle™

Question 55

If your colleagues were asked to describe your attitude, what would they share?

_____

_____

_____

_____

_____

_____

_____

_____

_____

_____

_____

_____

_____

_____

Question 56

Do you allow things in your life that are negative? Do they benefit you in any way?

Question 57

What do you need right now in your life?

Question 58

Who can you help today?

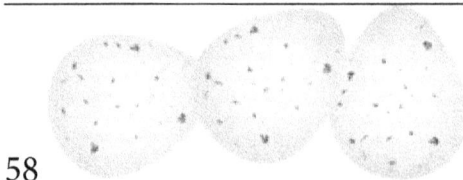

The Speckled Egg Principle™

Question 59

How do you define a fulfilled life? Are you there?

Question 60

Do you have a dream? Are you actively pursuing your dream?

Question 61

Who has influenced you the most in the past decade?

Question 62

What do you want your legacy to be?

Question 63

Do you dance in the rain?

Question 64

What holds you back?

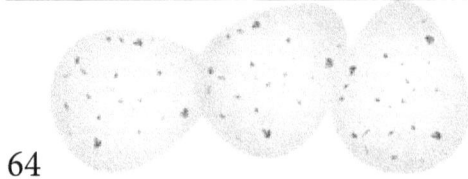

Question 65

What or who is your motivation?

Question 66

How do you define humility?

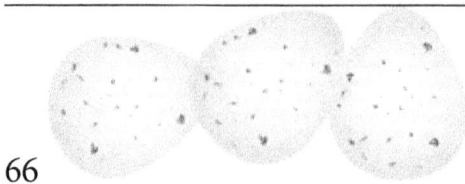

The Speckled Egg Principle™

Question 67

Do you live with passion?

Question 68

When have you had a dream come true?

The Speckled Egg Principle™

Question 69

What difference have you made today?

Question 70

What makes your heart sing?

Question 71

What is your personal brand? Is it your brand by design or by default? How do your choices impact your brand?

Question 72

If you wrote a book, what would the title be? Describe the main character.

Question 73

Are you equipped to do your best? What do you need? Do you know where to find it?

Carol J. Cline

Question 74

Is good enough, good enough?

The Speckled Egg Principle™

Question 75

How do you prioritize your work?

_____
_____
_____
_____
_____
_____
_____
_____
_____
_____
_____
_____
_____
_____
_____

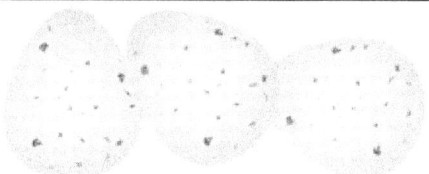

Question 76

Given the opportunity to be in a face-to-face meeting with the CEO and ask two questions (without any repercussions), what would they be?

_____
_____
_____
_____
_____
_____
_____
_____
_____
_____
_____
_____
_____
_____
_____

The Speckled Egg Principle™

Question 77

Does fear keep you from your dream?

Question 78

Where are you most "at home"?

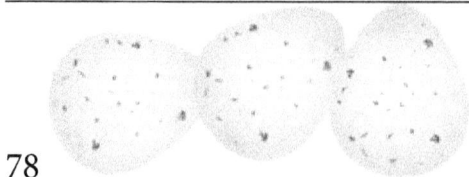

Question 79

If your heart wanders, where does it go?

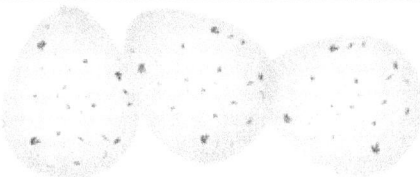

Question 80

What defines you?

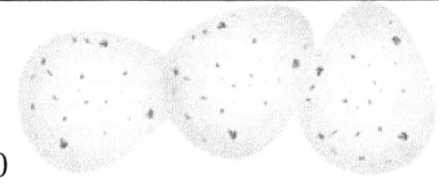

The Speckled Egg Principle™

Question 81

When you get to where you are going, where will you be?

Question 82

Is the invisible bandage over your struggles helping them to heal or just keeping them covered?

The Speckled Egg Principle™

Question 83

Are you growing? How have you grown this year?

_____
_____
_____
_____
_____
_____
_____
_____
_____
_____
_____
_____
_____
_____
_____
_____

Question 84

To whom would you will your attitude?

Question 85

What room in your house is your favorite?

Question 86

Why not...?

The Speckled Egg Principle™

Question 87

Are you a leader because of what you do or who you are? Are you more engaged in process or purpose?

Question 88

How will you use your talents in the next month? Year?

_____
_____
_____
_____
_____
_____
_____
_____
_____
_____
_____
_____
_____
_____

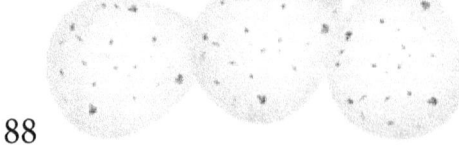

The Speckled Egg Principle™

Question 89

Do you trust your intuition?

Question 90

What triggers a defensive posture?

The Speckled Egg Principle™

Question 91

How many of the things you worry about actually happen?

Question 92

Who is your dearest confidant?

_____
_____
_____
_____
_____
_____
_____
_____
_____
_____
_____
_____
_____
_____
_____
_____

Question 93

Name ten things for which you are grateful.

Question 94

Who is your role model? What is that person's greatest attribute?

The Speckled Egg Principle™

Question 95

What does it mean to be a "person of character"?

Question 96

When was the last time you laughed so hard you cried?

The Speckled Egg Principle™

Question 97

Are most of your relationships meaningful or superficial? Which do you prefer?

Question 98

Do you prefer team or individual sports/activities/games?

The Speckled Egg Principle™

Question 99

What skill or talent would you like to develop?

Carol J. Cline

Question 100

When all is said and done, what will you have said? What will you have done?

Hatched

List the talents, skills, and gifts you currently use.

_____

_____

_____

_____

_____

_____

_____

_____

_____

_____

_____

Carol J. Cline

Incubate

List additional talents, skills, and gifts revealed in your answers.

_____

_____

_____

_____

_____

_____

_____

_____

_____

_____

Carol J. Cline

Nurture

In HATCHED and INCUBATE, you identified your speckled eggs. Are there some that would benefit from intentional development? Transfer those to this page.

_____
_____
_____
_____
_____
_____
_____
_____
_____

Carol J. Cline

Treasure Mapping & IT

What is Treasure Mapping?

Treasure Mapping is the intentional application of your speckled eggs. When you map your treasures, you are using your talents to make a difference in your world. Placing your treasures throughout environments — your home, workplace, neighborhood, outreach organizations, etc.— will enrich each in a variety of positive ways.

What is IT?

IT is the combination of Individual Talents that are uniquely you. You identified many of them on the HATCHED, INCUBATE, and NURTURE pages.

What difference does IT make?

What difference do your individual talents make to you personally, professionally, in your community, and to your organization?

Personally—Recognizing your unique talents will cause you as a person and a leader to be more fulfilled. Balanced. Energized.

Professionally—Working at a high level of personal satisfaction results in maximum contribution at work.

Community — When you display authentic leadership, you inspire others to do the same.

Organization — Everyone has value and needs to be equipped, encouraged, and empowered for the greatest contribution from and for all.

Complete this sentence. IT makes a difference because _____

_____

_____

_____

_____

How can IT be developed?

Optimize or create opportunities within the organization that allow you to develop a mutually beneficial skill or talent.

Observe people whose talents are further developed in the area you want to improve. Start a dialogue. Take lessons. Practice. Other:

_____

_____

Why should you celebrate IT?

You are uniquely gifted. Your Individual Talents shape you as a leader, as a person. You are in a position to influence outcomes. You have a platform as a leader to encourage and equip others to be their best. Your contributions inspire others.

Celebration and appreciation breed a culture of possibility and purposeful growth.

Inspire daily.

Conclusion

It is my hope that you will apply *The Speckled Egg Principle*™ in all areas of your life. May your speckled eggs reflect your values, heighten your joy, and create sustainable balance every day in every way. May you lead with intention. May you be true to yourself, your principles, and your dreams. And may others be inspired to do likewise.

About the Author

To successful life consultant and author Carol J. Cline, speckled eggs are the talents, gifts, and skills hidden under the wings of your organization that—when discovered and nurtured—will help your organization soar to amazing heights.

Carol is a thought leader and visionary in leadership, healthcare, and front line business operations. An organization's greatest asset is its people. She believes that every person has value. Whether they provide value to an organization depends largely on a leader's commitment to equip, encourage, and empower them to be successful in the right role.

The Speckled Egg Principle™ is foundational to intentional discovery and proper allocation of human resources. Having the right person in the right place, doing the right task for the right reason, will yield the right results.

Carol is a speaker, consultant, and certified life coach. Her passion and enthusiasm are contagious. She inspires others to identify their purpose and lead authentically. Her engaging delivery from the stage or sitting around the table inspires and motivates people of all walks of life to go beyond "good enough."

Carol J. Cline

To bring *The Speckled Egg Principle*™ to your organization, please contact Carol directly.

Carol J. Cline
Speaker, Coach, Consultant
PO Box 2236
Tarpon Springs, FL 34688-2236

Email: caroljcline@gmail.com
Website: www.thespeckledeggprinciple.com
Website: www.carolclineconsulting.com

www.ingramcontent.com/pod-product-compliance
Lightning Source LLC
Chambersburg PA
CBHW071521080526
44588CB00011B/1518